Text and Texture

Contemporary Calligraphic Paintings

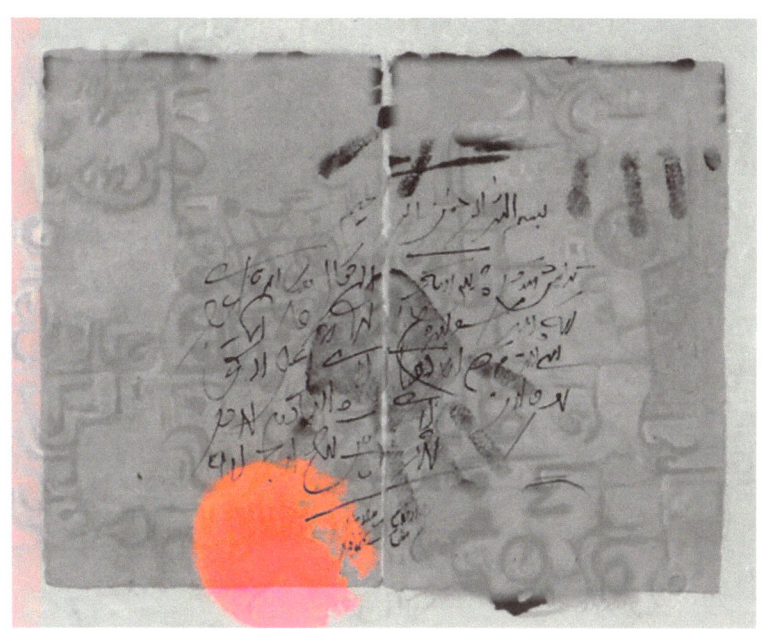

Rashid Arshed

Text and Texture

Text and Texture

Contemporary Calligraphic Paintings

Author Rashid Arshed

First Edition.

Copyright©2018 Rashid Arshed

Cover and Book Design by Rashid Arshed

All rights reserved. No part of the contents of this book

may be reproduced in any form or by any means without

the written permission of the Author.

First Edition

All Rights Reserved

Contemporary Calligraphic Paintings

The Evolution

Syed Amjad Ali

The work of Rashid Arshed is well known, both as an artist and a teacher of artists.

Together his onerous duties as Principal of the Central Institute of Arts and Crafts, he has quietly but assiduously continued to paint, with that sincerity and devotion which is bound to produce results.

The result is a definite and new contribution to the art of Pakistan

As everyone knows, painting immediately after independence was dominated by figurative and traditional painters like Chughtai and Allah Bux, Askari and Shaikh Ahmed. Even the early entrant like Sadequain and Guljee followed the figurative style.

The scene was then invaded by young modernists including Parvez and Ai Imam, Shemza and Safdar. Zubaida Agha and Shakir Ali were already there, adding to the strength of the movement.

Text and Texture

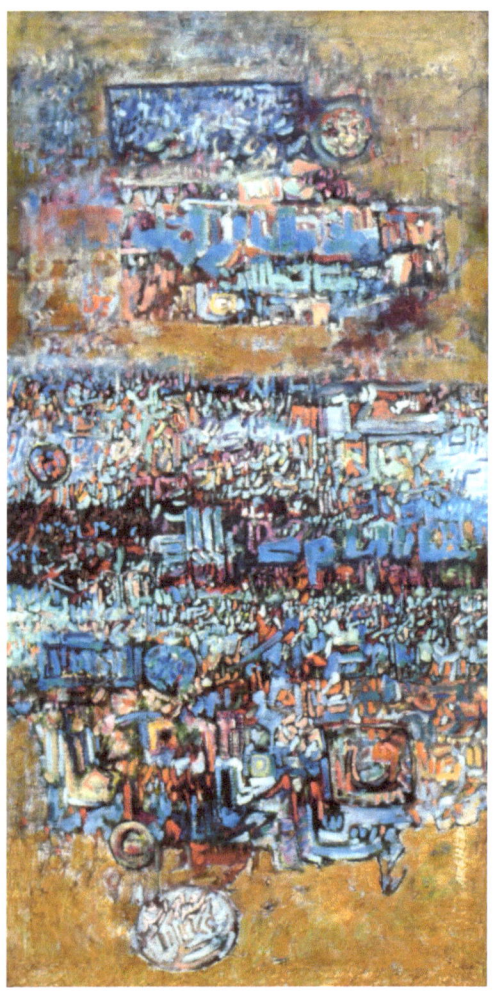

April 74, Oil on Canvas. Ayesha Arshed and Saleem Arshed, USA.

Soon the work of modern artist became quite mature and claimed admiration from everyone, but there were nagging doubts in the minds of many as to the genuineness of the contribution by our artists, for the work they produced was like any that could be seen in Paris, New York or Tokyo.

At first the Pakistani artists fiercely defended their ground but feeling in their heart the justice of criticism, they looked around for ways to introduce a Pakistani element in their work.

At this stage, the most honoured of our traditional arts came to our help namely, calligraphy. Hanif Ramay was perhaps the first to try to make a painting out of calligraphy, but the work was rather immature. Shakir introduce calligraphy as part of a full-fledged mural which he did for PINSTECH in Islamabad. Sadequain took to great heights by actually writing Quranic and poetical texts in a unique style, with addition of colours and some decoration. Many others followed.

Contemporary Calligraphic Paintings

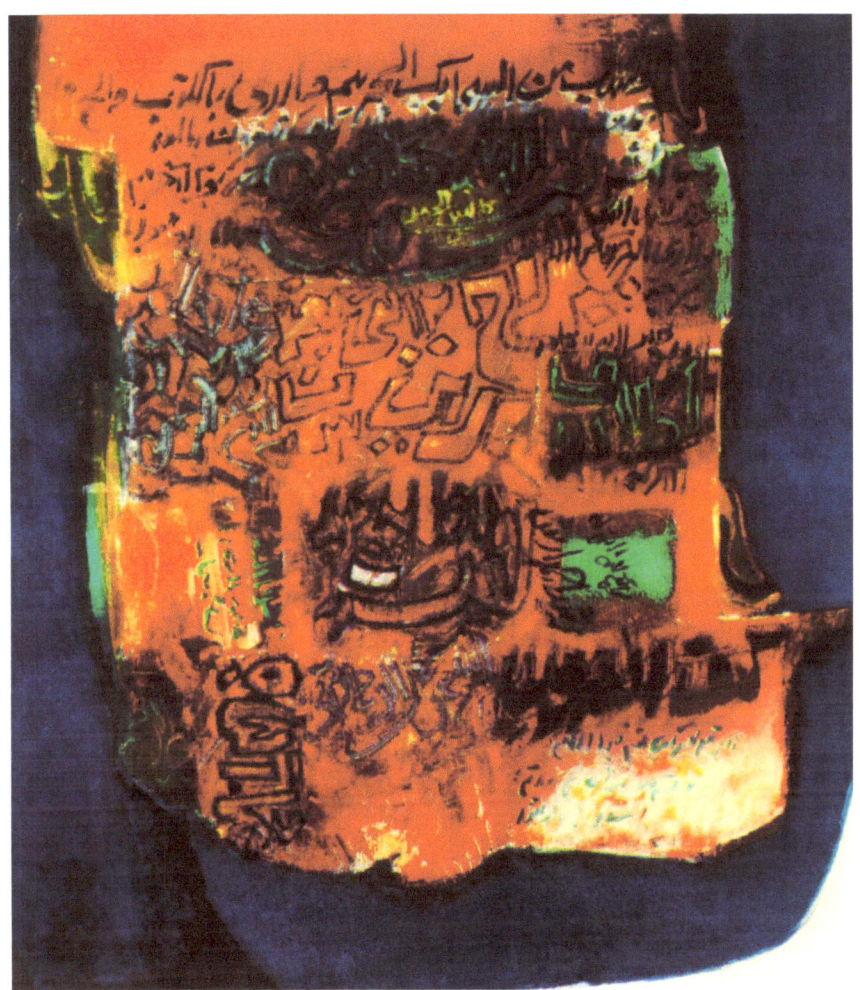

Untitled, 1971, Oil on Canvas, EFU Insurance, Karachi.

Text and Texture

But it was left to Rashid Arshed to use calligraphy as theme in his paintings. He does not practice calligraphy. He uses the beautiful effects produced by masterpieces of calligraphy as the subject of his paintings, like another artist uses trees or birds or apples or faces or fabric.

In his paintings we are reminded of old *Farmans* of Kings, inscriptions, on historical monuments, beautiful old manuscripts, and other master pieces of the art of writing.

He uses the look, the feeling, the atmosphere, of the writing as the subject of the painting. It is a creative and not a passive use of calligraphy, because he is not repeating any style or even his style of writing, but introducing new elements to the bare and austere linier rhythms of writing, so as to make it painting.

He places writing in space, with light and shadow, tone

Untitled, 1992, Oil on Canvas, Private Collection.

Contemporary Calligraphic Paintings

and tint, just like any other object. Some letters are projecting, some receding; some dim, some clear; some ponderous, some light and airy; some curvilinear, some angular.

The whole subject is composed on the canvas, with a certain background, diagonally or vertically or in any other way.

If calligraphy came in to give a Pakistani touch to our painting, here calliraphy has been transformed for the first time into a painting not merely by colouring the letters but by using them as subject of a painting, complete with space and atmosphere. This is a new ground broken by Arshed and it is a definite step forward in the growth of Pakistani Art.

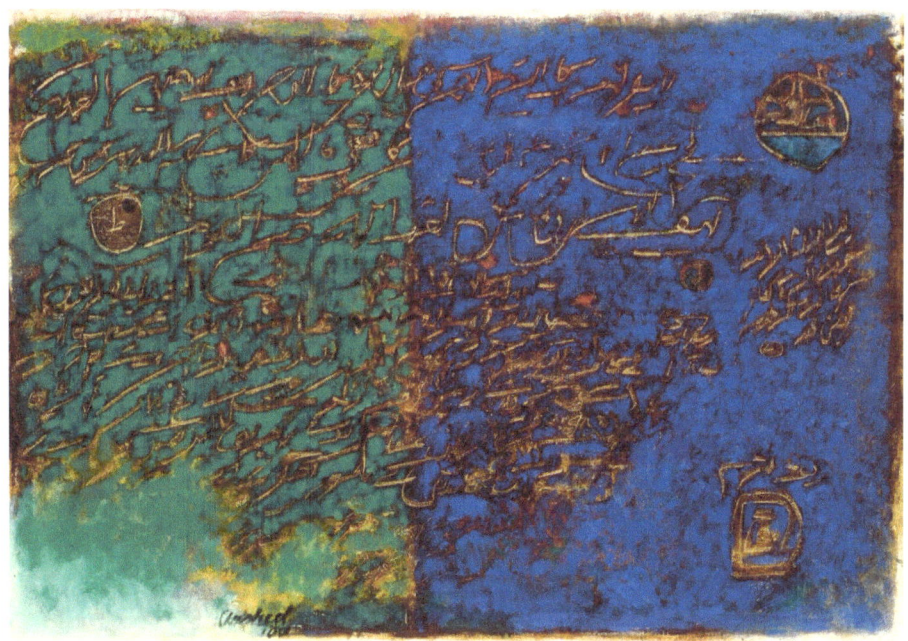

Love Letter, Oil on Canvas, Private Collection.

Text and Texture

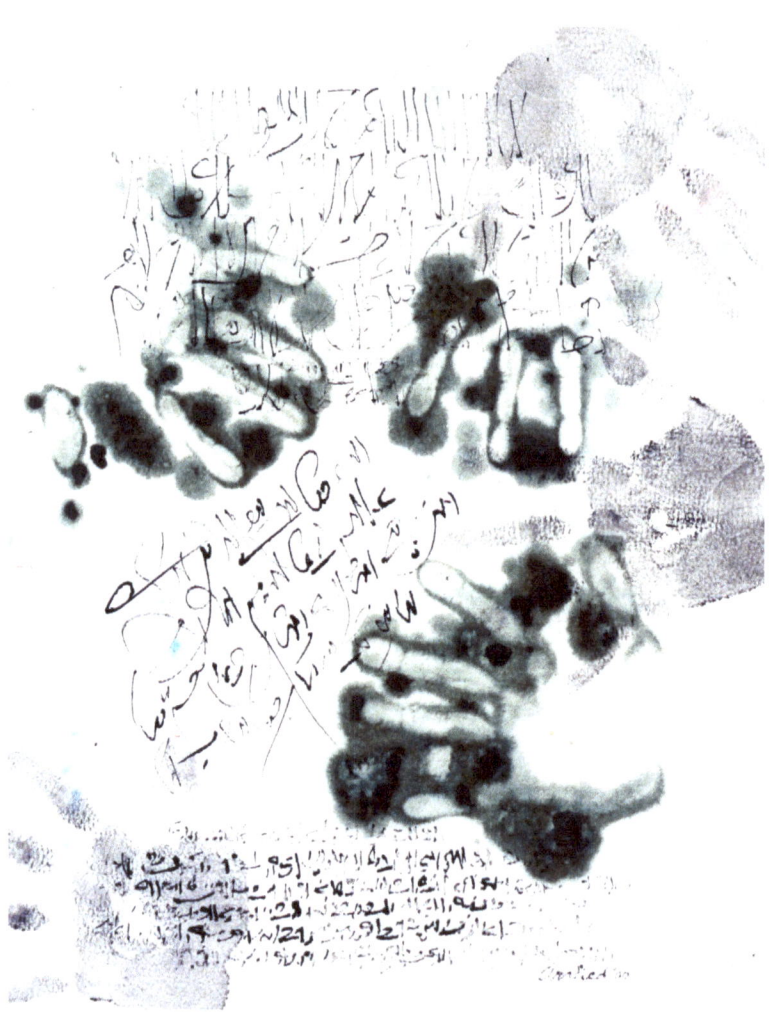

These Hands, Linen Pulp Painting, 2000., Private Collection.

Lines of Desire and Destiny

Quddus Mirza

There have been artists in our midst who not only explored the aesthetic possibilities of script in their art but also were writers and poets. These include Anwar Jalal Shemza, Sadequain, Haneef Ramay, Tassadaq Suhail and to an extent Shakir Ali.

Rashid Arshed belongs to that group of artists who are well-versed in both -- the art of writing and writing -- and have pursued them both equally seriously. He has published a number of books; his latest, Jungle mein Mangal is a collection of humorous essays in Urdu. Having obtained his "Diploma in Art" from the Mayo School of Art in 1960, he was appointed the principal of Central School of Arts and Craft, Karachi in 1970. He left his teaching position in 1975, and migrated to the US. After spending many years there, he returned to Pakistan in 2006 and became the Head of Fine Arts at the Indus Valley School of Art and Architecture in Karachi for a period of two years.

All these biographical details may appear extraneous, but are essential in order to comprehend the man behind the painter Rashid Arshed. His fascination with script, as a mode of creative expression, has a peculiar history, besides being a personal passion. This is long before calligraphic painting became a politically- and economically-correct pursuit during

Text and Texture

Black Page, Linen Pulp Painting, 2000, Noorjehan and Aqeel Bilgrami, Karachi

Contemporary Calligraphic Paintings

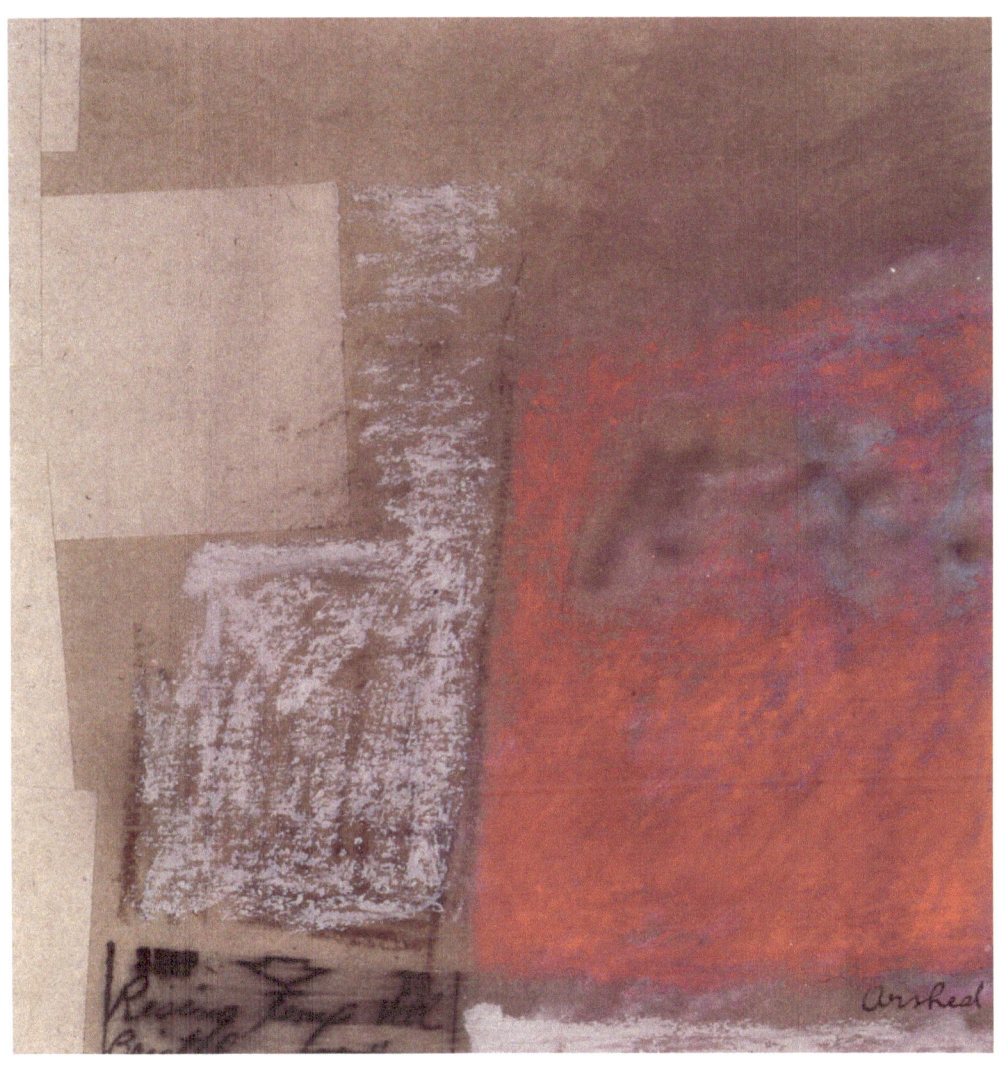

Aesthetic Probe 2, 1992, Brown Paper and Oil Sticks

Text and Texture

the military dictatorship of General Zia.

Arshed stood apart from this crowd of opportunity-seekers, since his connection with calligraphy was genuine. To begin with, it was his literary inclination that provided a subject in the form of text. While the writer managed language in his books, the painter manipulated words for pictorial purposes. Thus his work, from an early stage, was about text-based surfaces, built with layers of letters, which in most cases were indecipherable or indistinguishable. Richly tactile canvases conveyed the presence of script but the aspect of readability was altered for visual effect.

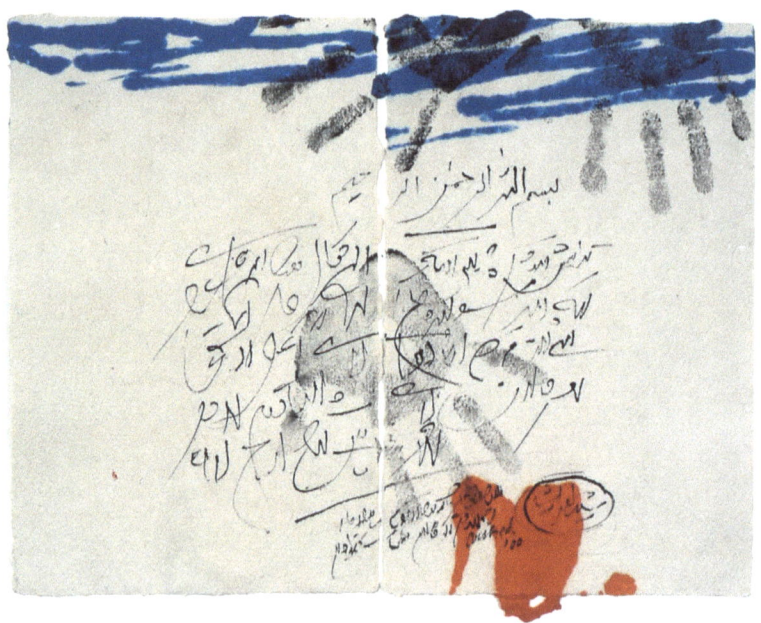

My Dear Friend, Linen Pulp Painting, 2000, Private Collection

Contemporary Calligraphic Paintings

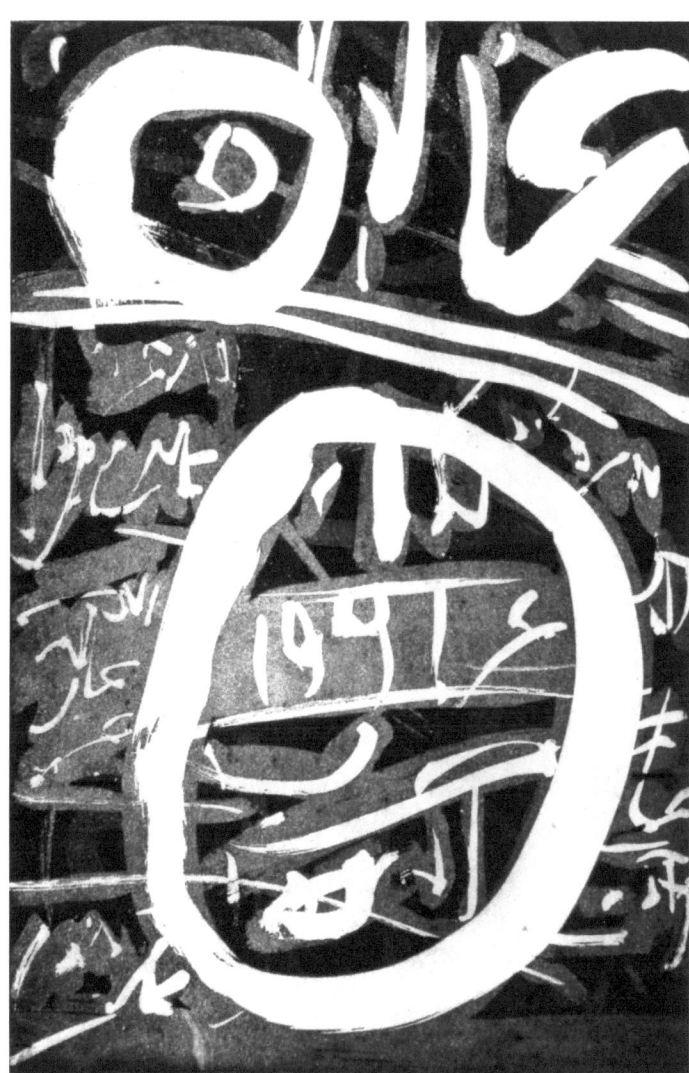

Insignia, Engraving, 1991.

Text and Texture

In almost every painting, the words are not drawn clearly; on the other hand, they look like shapes that have some link with the written language, not necessarily Arabic (in a few paintings the nature of text reminds one of the script of ancient civilizations.

In other works, too, one finds it difficult to decipher alphabets; so one has to search for meanings behind these marks. It is slightly easier to catch the name of God and Holy Prophet, even though these are constructed as abstract images. Besides these single-word paintings, most others offer clues to sacred script, without revealing much. This tendency to veil the word, the Word of God, may have multiple connotations. It certifies the painterly approach employed in treating text as a visual texture. At the same time, it affirms the sacred substance of being a code that needs to be located and understood after effort and time. In a way the energy spent in searching, reading and unfolding the text serves as some sort of a spiritual experience -- enhanced with a careful arrangement of contrasting colours and vivid hues. These shades merge with each other in a subtle manner, adding to the illusion of a harmonious activity -- a mantra -- that can be invoked by gazing at the paintings for a longer span.

The art of Rashid Arshed affirms that the artist can liberate himself from restrictions of all sorts; his work may also serve to free a viewer's perception about art, religion and politics, components of our culture that were inseparable in the past but not anymore.

First published in The News, Karachi

Calling on Calligraphy

Rashid Arshed

The Icon, Acrylic on Canvas, 2000. Private Collection,

After World War II, a number of Islamic countries won their independence from Western Colonial rule. In all these countries, European art traditions had taken root. With the perception of freedom, the young artists of these countries began to look towards their own cultural roots and a large number of artists turned to traditional Islamic calligraphy for inspiration.

In Pakistan, Hanif Ramey is known to be the first to use calligraphy in his paintings in the Fifties. He used the *Kalima* and short verses of the Qur'an in different styles and colors. Sadequain's calligraphic paintings stem from his unique personal handwriting. Zahoourl Akhlaq and Rashid Arshed gave a new meaning to the art of calligraphy by using the elements of calligraphy to construct contemporary compositions. Ahmed Khan from the same group relied on the verses of the Holy Quran by oxidizing

Text and Texture

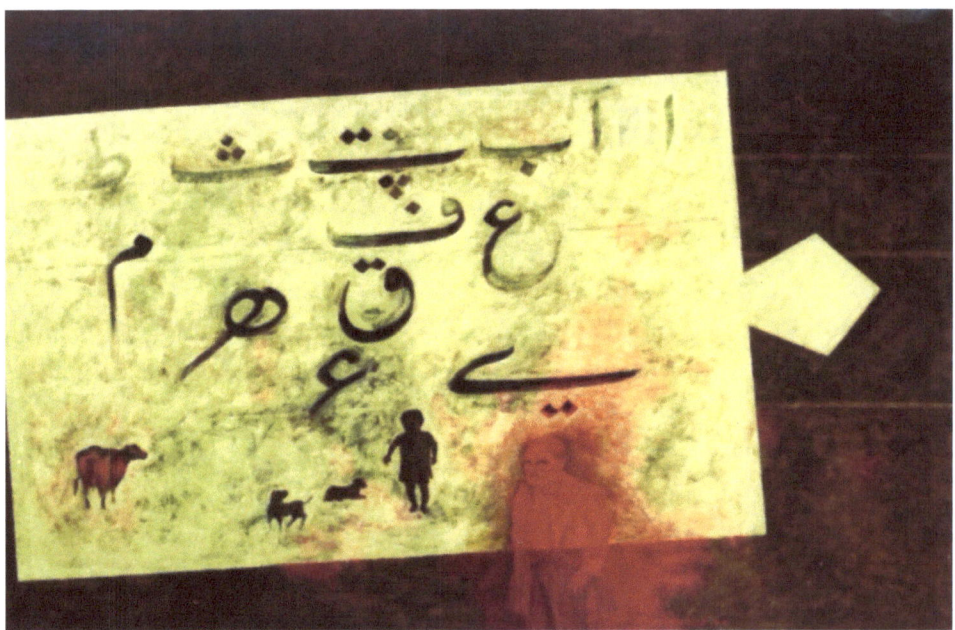

Autobiography, Acrylic on Canvas, 2000. Rashida and Aftab Tapal, Karachi.

> *My practice of writing Takhti (wooden tablet) began in my mother's lap. Perpetual practice together with exposure to vernacular literature, Books and old manuscripts developed into a love and admiration of the art of beautiful writing.*

Contemporary Calligraphic Paintings

aluminum sheets, and creating a plethora of colors. Shakir Ali also did some remarkable calligraphic paintings, banking on his cubist style and background in textile design. Ismail Guljee skillfully turned the serene and disciplined art of calligraphy into abstract expression or action painting.

Shemza's paintings are based on Islamic geometric patterns showing the distinct influence of Paul Klee. Jamil Naqsh joined the fold much later with extensive work in calligraphic paintings, employing the richly-crafted textures that he cultivated over a period of many years, which he used skillfully in his "Woman and Pigeon" paintings. Mehar Afroz is yet another artist in this long list. What is surprising that, although contemporary calligraphy has been in practice for more than half a century, and across a large geographically region cov-

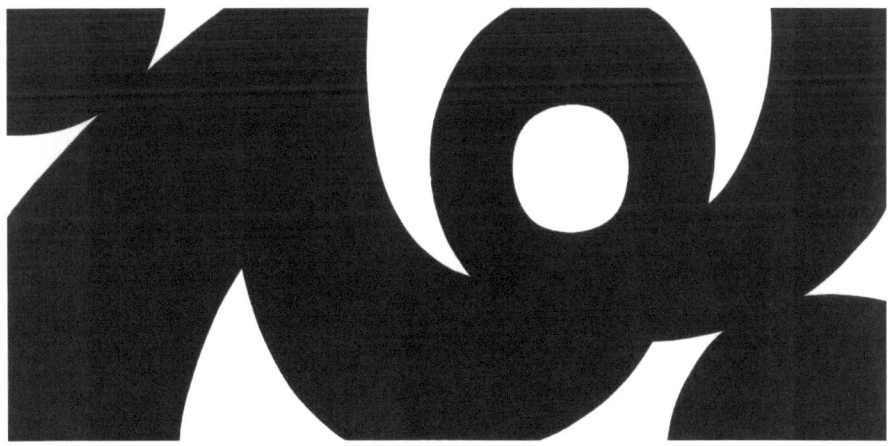

Reclining Figure, Acrylic on Canvas, 2006

Text and Texture

ering North Africa, the Middle East and South Asia, this popular genre has not acquired the status of a movement.

My practice of writing *Takhti* (wooden tablet) began in my mother's lap. Perpetual practice together with exposure to vernacular literature, Books and old manuscripts developed into a love and admiration of the art of beautiful writing.

In 1970 I had a solo exhibition at the American Center, Karachi, based exclusively on my calligraphic paintings. Because of the use of calligraphy, the show was titled "The Manuscript." The paintings were also titled accordingly; as Preface, Page One, Page Two and Epilogue, etc. From the very beginning, instead of readable text, I have been using the elements of calligraphy to explore the aesthetics and to capture its spirit.

Since then, I have consistently

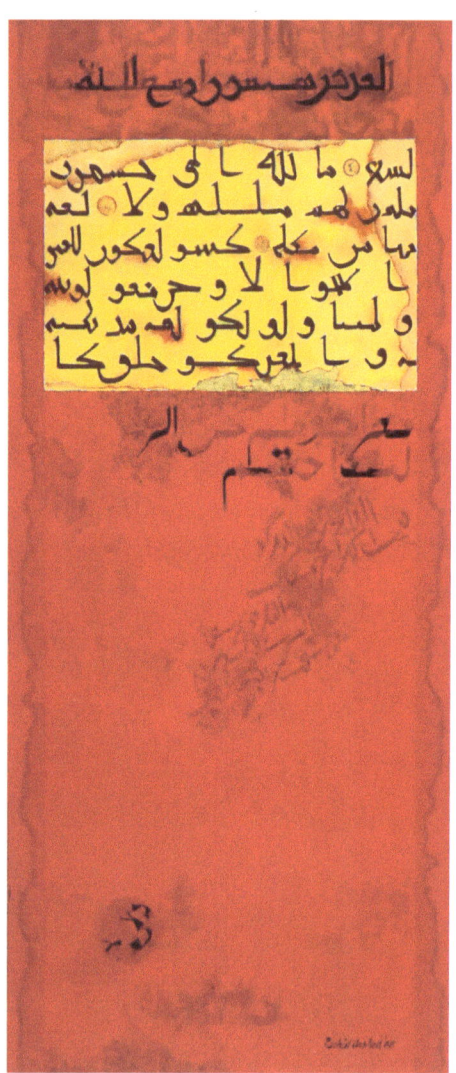

Tradition and Transition 2, Oil on Canvas, 2008.
Private Collection.

Contemporary Calligraphic Paintings

used calligraphy as a mode of expression. In doing so, I have tried to answer a question of fundamental importance. How does a contemporary calligraphic painting differ from traditional calligraphy? The question is not about which one is better or superior. The traditional Islamic calligraphy with innumerable styles *(Khat)* evolved since the rise of Islam and reached the epitome of grace and beauty during the Ottoman period.

There are several factors which need to be kept in mind when we examine the traditional calligraphy and contemporary calligraphic paintings. Notwithstanding innumerable variations and innovations in each style, a traditional calligrapher is restricted by the rigid discipline that has been handed down for centuries. In many scripts precise measurements are required when executing horizontal, vertical and diagonal strokes or a cur-

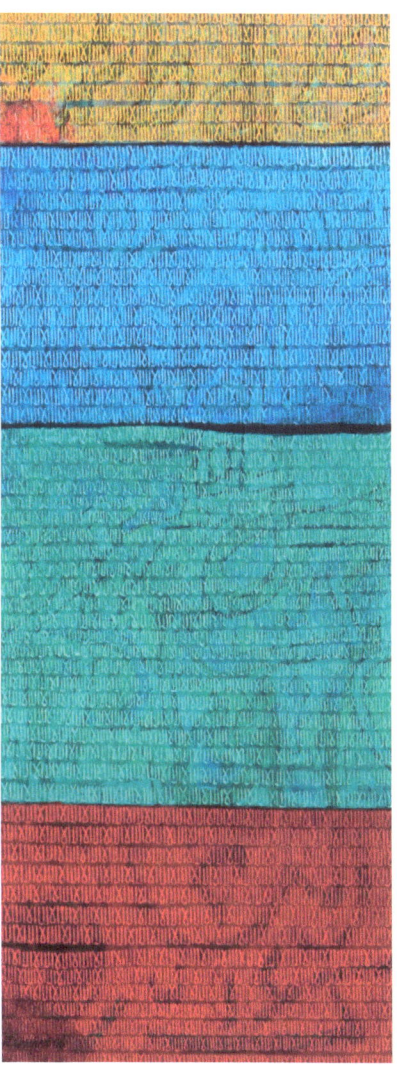

In Essence 10, Acrylic on Canvas, 2006, Sayyeda Habib, Karachi.

Text and Texture

vilinear form. It would be correct to assert that a geometric grid, visible or invisible, is followed in many styles. This discipline is achieved through rigorous eye and hand training. On the other hand, a contemporary artist has unrestricted freedom to break the barriers of tradition and push the boundaries of creativity to the best of his capacity. His palette and his canvas, in literal and in metaphorical terms, are as vast as his imagination. This freedom also lends to a variety of expressions – from painterly to abstract and from impressionistic to expressionistic.

God created man in his own image, say the Scriptures. It is natural, then, that the creation partakes of the attributes or qualities of the Creator. A child reflects traits from his parents. Likewise, a work or art also personifies the artist. Depending on the nature and temperament of the artist, his

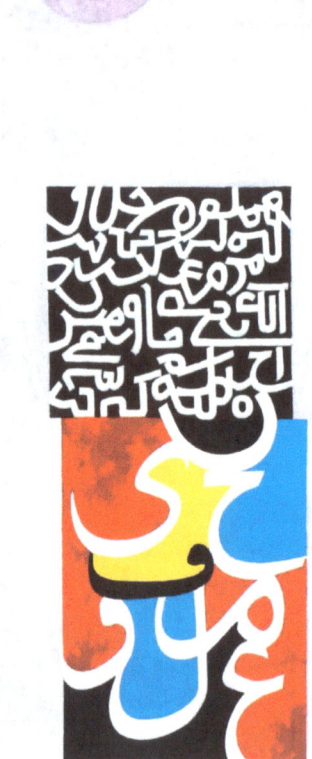

Tradition and Transition 7., Acrylic on Canvas, 2008. Hundal Collection (Shireen and Afzal Ahmad, Chicago).

Contemporary Calligraphic Paintings

In Essence 13, Acrylic on Canvas, 2006. Hundal Collection (Shireen and Afzal Ahmad, Chicago).

work can be serene, emotive, evocative, provocative or something else altogether. This personification is the identity of the artist. The subject matter also plays a role in arousing feelings of one kind or another.

For me, the subject of Calligraphy is expression of peace, serenity and spiritualism. The inherent mystic quality of the Arabic characters, together with chromatic, tactile and spatial dispensations, imbues a spiritual aura into a calligraphic painting and the act of painting itself becomes meditative.

Elements of Space and Silence

How often have I felt lonely and detached in a crowd, yet surrounded by thoughts when I am in a state of solitude!

Ghalib, the famous Urdu poet, has captured these feelings in the following couplet:

Man is a concourse of thoughts within himself. What we think of as a crowd could be my privacy.

The 'Privacy' that Ghalib refers to can also be described as silence. Silence is often soothing but at times it can be vivid and agitating. In a musical composition, silence is referred to as a pause, that I consider the most pleasant or effective musical note.

In art and design, silence, in the strictest sense of the word, is generally conveyed through unused space. Nonetheless, a field of color or a textured plane can also be termed as space. What we refer to as 'unused' space is, in fact, that which is 'best used' by a creative mind. In literature, space is defined

Contemporary Calligraphic Paintings

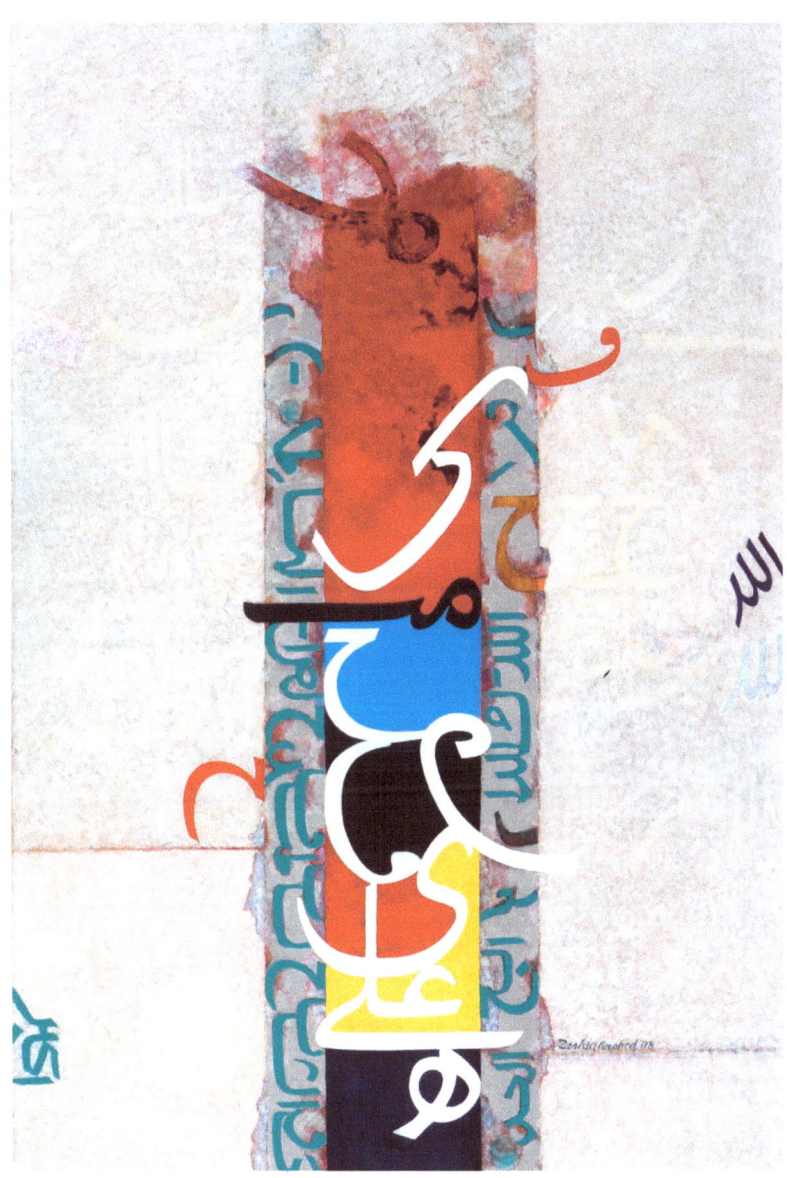

Tradition and Transition 16, Acrylic on Canvas, 2008. Rashida and Aftab Tapal, Karachi.

Text and Texture

as abstract thought, a message, or a background, as opposed to time or narrative.

Space brings the subject in focus, emphasizing its presence and importance in relation to its surroundings. In many of my paintings, I've addressed the challenge of space in more than one way, ranging from simple monochromatic planes to textured surface. I enjoy maintaining the critical and profound relationship between used and unused space and have employed the concept distinctively in most of my paintings.

All of us will have imbibed the true love for the great art of calligraphy in all its various aspects from the beginning, when the written word was created by man as the only and greatest sign which distinguishes man from his fellow creatures, and in this veneration of the work, I feel all of us are united.

Dr. Annemarie Schimmel

Text and Texture
Koel Gallery 2018

Whether it is a single letter, a word, or a document, it contains and reflects all the essential properties, or characteristics that entail beauty. And texture in a text is the total sum of form, space, rhythm and other elements that contribute to aesthetics of a unit. Therefore, the entire body of my calligraphic paintings, since my first showing at the American Center in Karachi in 1970 come under the umbrella of text and texture. It is for the same reason that I have titled the catalogue of my current exhibition at Koel Gallery as Text and Texture.

Text and Texture 9, Oil on Canvas, 2013, 22x48 inches.

Text and Texture

Text and Texture 22, 2018, Oil on Canvas, 72x24 inches

Life is a learning experience, as they say, and after nearly 60 years of dabling in paint, I am still holding the brush and pallete in my hand, hopeing to kindle some new fire.

Text and Texture 3, Acrylic on Canvas, 2013, 48x22 inches.

Contemporary Calligraphic Paintings

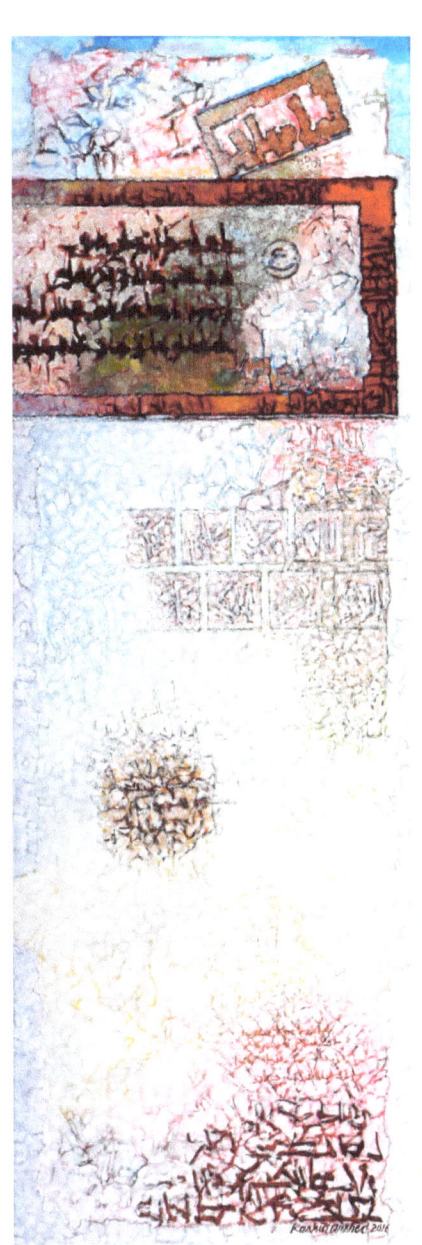

Text and Texture 16, Oil on Canvas, 2013, 58x20 inches

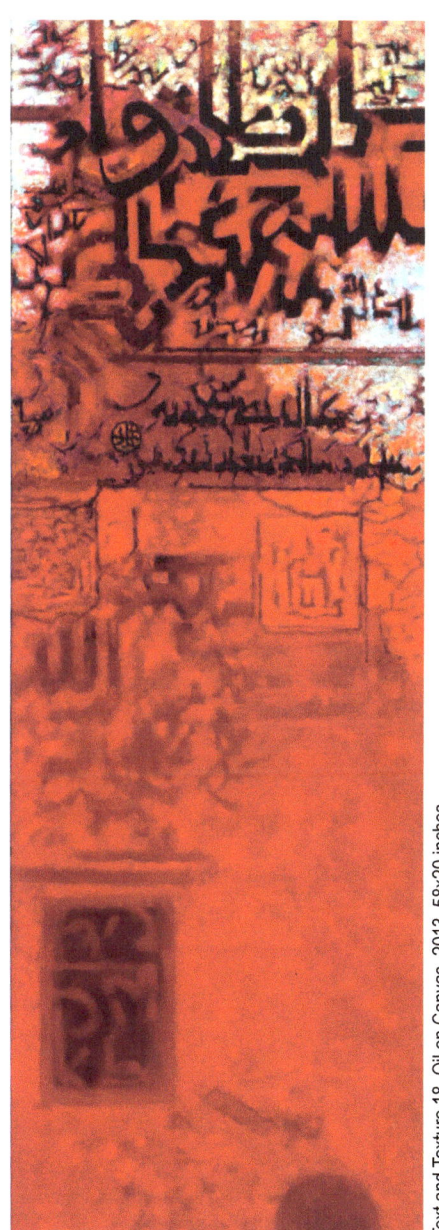

Text and Texture 18, Oil on Canvas, 2013, 58x20 inches

Text and Texture

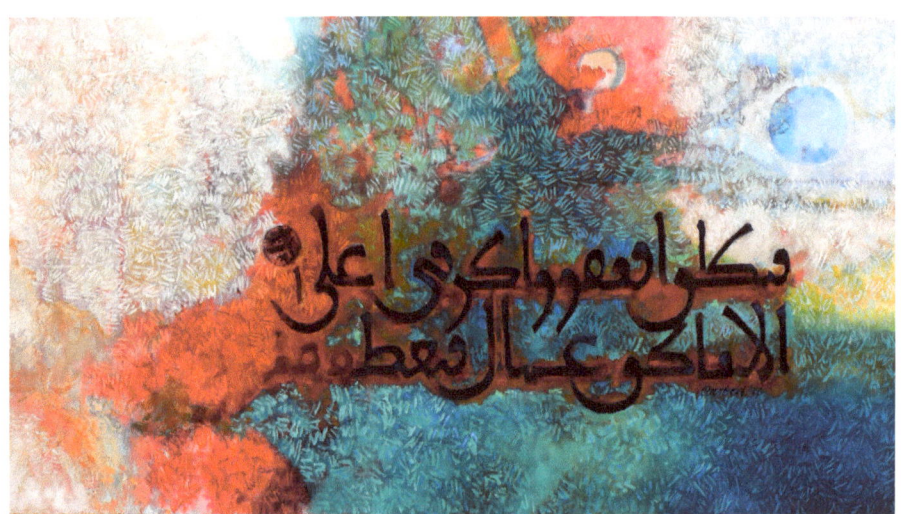

Text and Texture 13, Oil on Canvas, 2016, 24x48 inches.

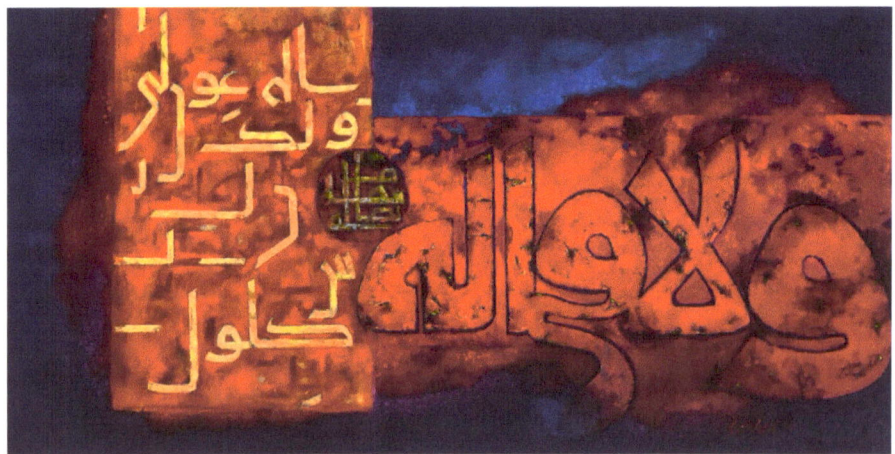

Text and Texture 8, Oil on Canvas, 2013, 22x48 inches.

Contemporary Calligraphic Paintings

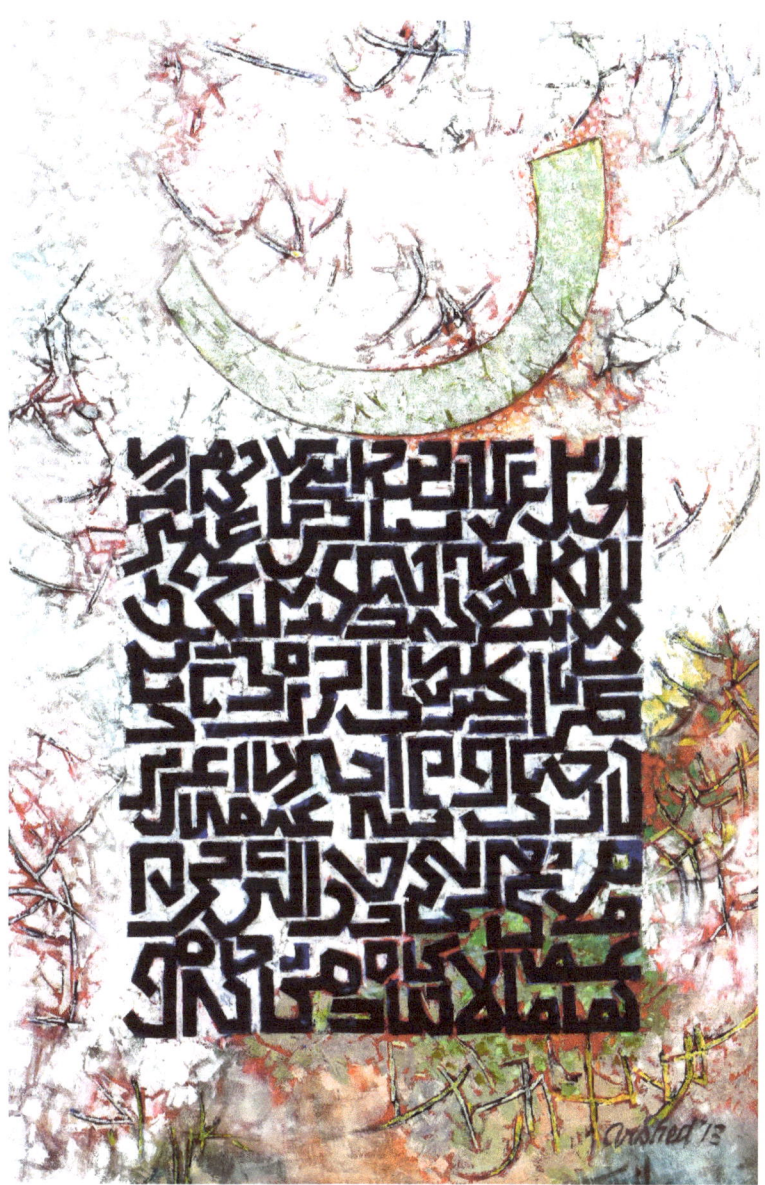

Text and Texture 5, Oil on Canvas, 2013, 36x24 inches.

Text and Texture

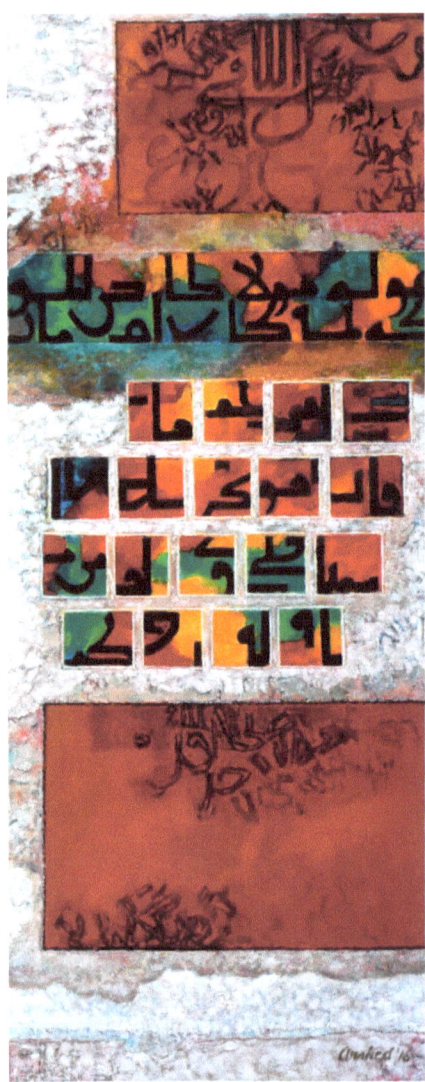

Text and Texture 10, Oil on Canvas, 2013, 54x22 inches

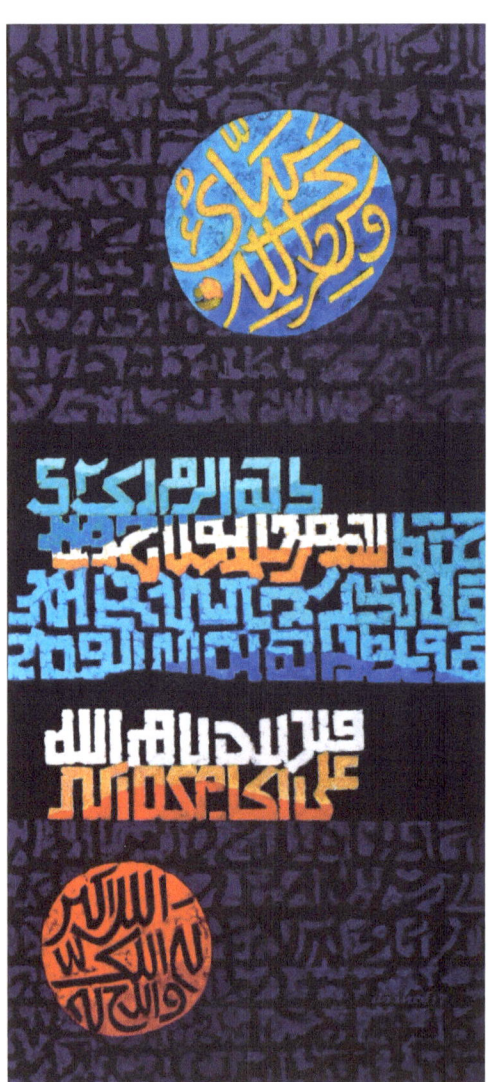

Text and Texture 17, Acrylic on Canvas, 2013, 48x24

Contemporary Calligraphic Paintings

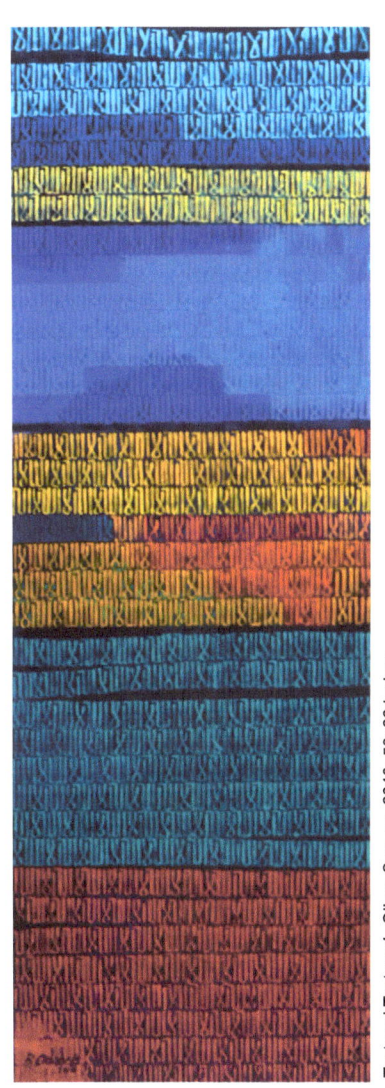

Text and Texture 1, Oil on Canvas, 2013, 58x22 inches

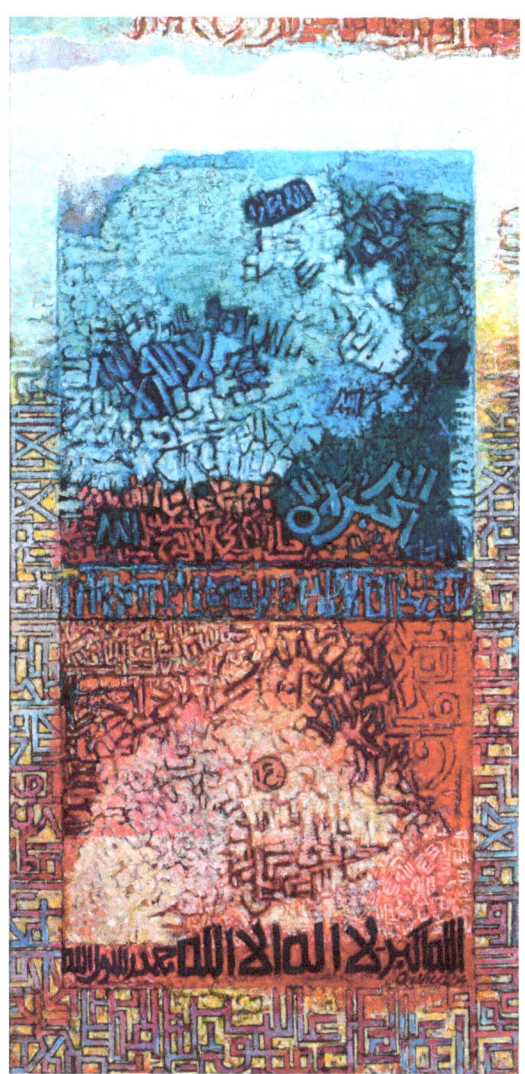

Text and Texture 6, Oil on Canvas, 2013, 48x24 inches

Text and Texture

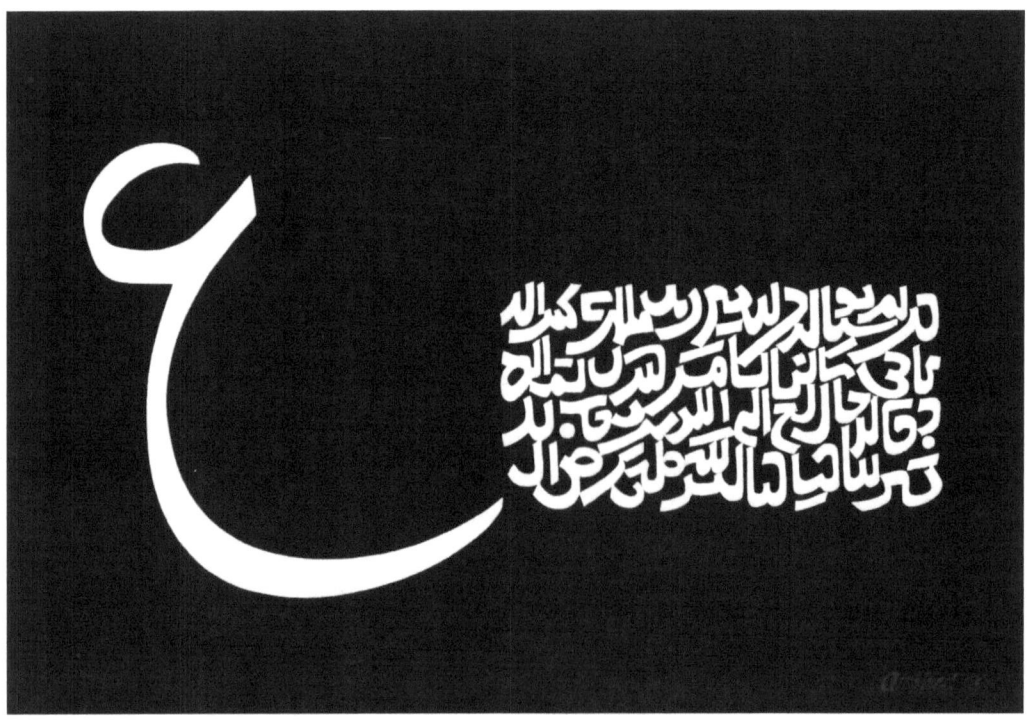

Text and Texture 2, Acrylic on Canvas, 2013, 36x24 inches.

Contemporary Calligraphic Paintings

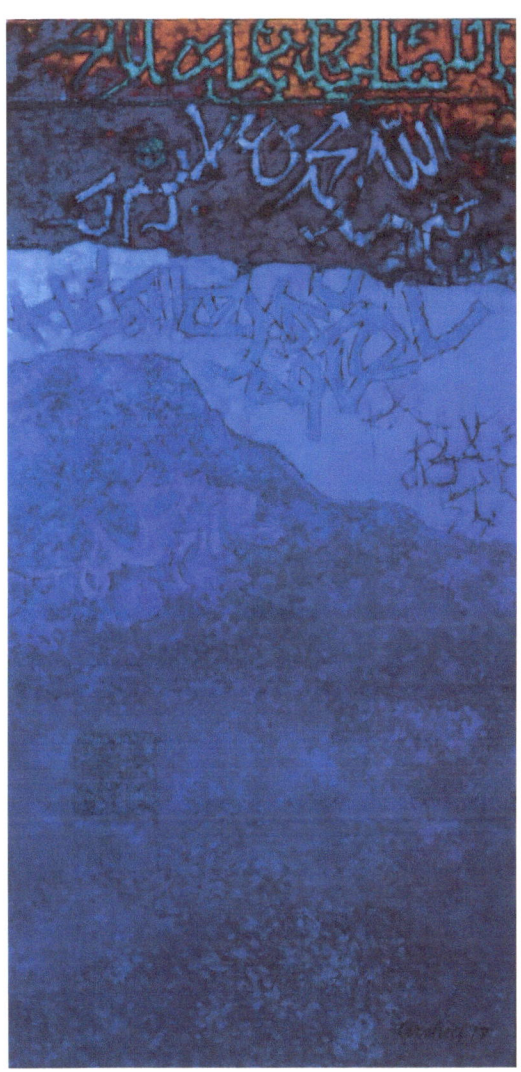

Text and Texture 19, Oil on Canvas, 2016, 48x24 inches

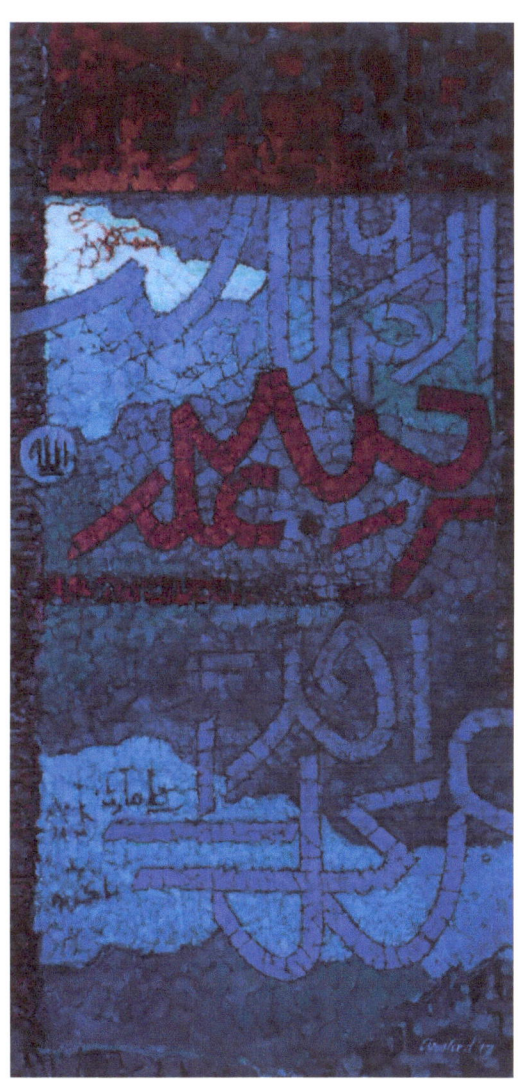

Text and Texture 20, Oil on Canvas, 2016, 48x24 inches

Text and Texture

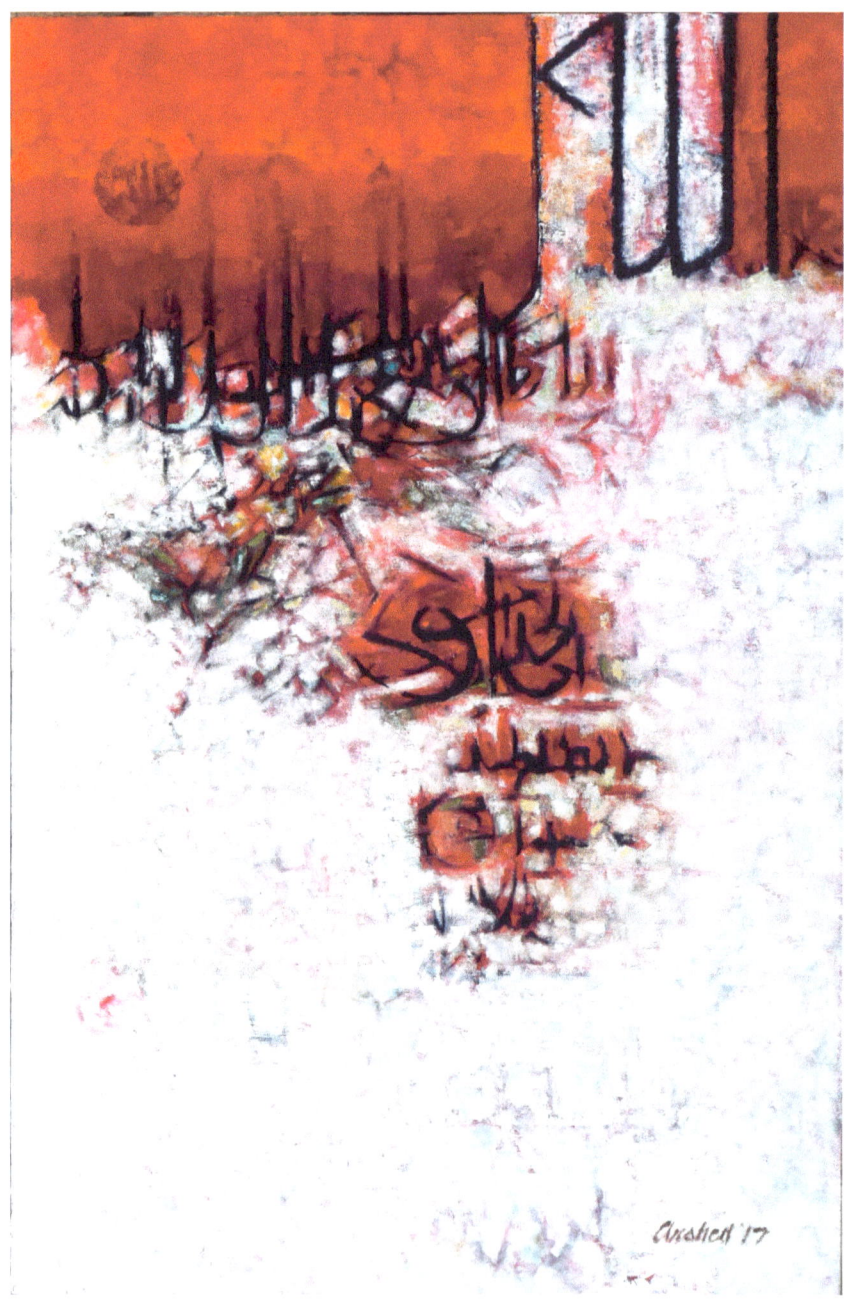

Text and Texture 21, Oil on Canvas, 2017, 36x24 inches.

www.ingramcontent.com/pod-product-compliance
Lightning Source LLC
Chambersburg PA
CBHW051819210526
45473CB00005B/1668